MY Dad makes the BEST boats!

Routledge
Taylor & Francis Group

LONDON AND NEW YORK

First published 2012 by Speechmark Publishing Ltd.

Published 2017 by Routledge
2 Park Square, Milton Park, Abingdon, Oxon OX14 4RN
711 Third Avenue, New York, NY 10017, USA

Routledge is an imprint of the Taylor & Francis Group, an informa business

British Library Cataloguing in Publication Data
A catalogue record for this book is available from the British Library

ISBN 9780863889882 (pbk)

MY Dad makes the BEST boats!

Routledge
Taylor & Francis Group

LONDON AND NEW YORK

NOTES FOR PARENTS

Parents who have a brain injury and their partners often ask, "how can we talk to our children about brain injury?" The answer is straightforward: you can talk to them about it in the same way that you talk to them about all other aspects of your lives as a family.

Honesty is vital; children always know if things are being kept from them and consequently imagine things to be much worse. They need to know the facts about brain injury in a way that is relevant to them. Lots of children like to know about what happened and when if they were not old enough to remember. They need to know that they won't get a brain injury by just banging their head. They need reassurance that what has happened and the consequences are not their fault.

Your child needs to understand that it is not a terminal disease and they need to be given information about the most common issues after a brain injury like forgetting, reduced tolerance to noise and temper problems.

They need an opportunity to ask questions and to feel that it is all right to ask questions at any time in the future. As they get older they will want more information as their cognitive ability improves.

This book has been designed so that children of between five and eight can read it independently. However, ideally it should be used with an adult to facilitate discussion about all aspects of family life and to enhance general emotional wellbeing. The book deliberately makes brain injury one of many things going on for this small group of children because for most children it is only one of many issues in their family life.

The story is intended to emphasise that all families are different, with their own strengths and weaknesses and different experiences. Brain injury is another experience that some people encounter and others do not.

Use the book as a template to enable you to create your own family book that is personal to your family life. Together, create a book that includes the names and adventures of your family and the positive and negative experiences that brain injury creates.

Jo Johnson

Consultant Neuropsychologist

Other books by the same author include:

My Mum makes the best cakes
For younger children who have a Mum with a brain injury

"My Parent has a Brain Injury" ... a guide for young people
Aimed at older children and teenagers

Everyone in Mrs Rutter's class is very excited. Tomorrow is the children's boat race at the village stream. The race happens just once a year. The winner is the first boat to get to the bridge.

"Who made the winning boat last year?" asks Mrs Rutter.

"Oscar won last year," says Samuel, "because his Dad makes great boats!" Oscar smiles. He feels proud of his Dad.

"I wonder who'll win this year," says Mrs Rutter.

Do you like making things?

At bedtime Oscar and his Dad are reading a book together. Oscar's favourite book is about Rosie and Jim and their boat.

Dad and Oscar laugh at the picture of Rosie and Jim's boat crashing into the river bank.

"I hope my boat does not crash in the race," says Oscar.

"I forgot the race was tomorrow," Dad says.

"Oh Dad, you are always forgetting!" laughs Oscar.

Does your Dad forget things?

The boats are lined up ready to start the race.

All the Mums and Dads have come to watch. Mr Smart, the Head Teacher, shouts, "Ready, steady…"

"…GO!" shout all the children.

What is your teacher's name?

Oscar and Samuel run along the edge of the stream to follow their boats.

"Hooray!" shouts Oscar, "my boat is the winner!"

Oscar's Dad gives him a hug. "We make a good team Oscar," he says.

"Your Dad makes great boats," says Samuel.

Samuel feels sad. "I wish my Dad would help me, my boat always sinks!"

"Next year," says Oscar, "my Dad will help you too."

What makes you feel sad?

The boys walk home with Oscar's Dad

"I like walking with your Dad," says Samuel, "He walks slowly like us. My Dad goes too fast and I get left behind."

Oscar's Dad smiles, "I have to walk slowly, I get tired."

Does your Dad get tired?

Today is sports day.

Samuel, Georgina and Oscar's team win the egg and spoon race. They are very excited.

Samuel's Dad runs in the Dad's race but Oscar's Dad has a bad leg so he can't run in the race. Oscar and his Dad cheer for Samuel's Dad and clap when he wins.

"Why didn't your Dad run?" asks Samuel.

"He had a car crash when I was four and hurt his head. Now he has a brain injury," Oscar says.

What things does your Dad find difficult?

Georgina says, "I banged my head today, do I have a brain injury?" Oscar thinks that's funny.

The boys laugh. "Girls are so silly!"

Oscar tells his friends, "You don't get a brain injury from a little bump. My Dad hurt his head very badly in a big car crash. Now he has a bad leg, he forgets things and says the wrong words. Sometimes he gets cross or sad."

Do you talk to your friends about your Dad?

Oscar is eating his dinner. It's his favourite, chicken nuggets and chips.

"Mum?" he says, "at school I told Georgina and Samuel about Dad's car crash."

"That's great!" Mum answers.

"It is good to talk to your friends about what happened to Dad."

I wish Dad had not had his crash," says Oscar.

"So do I," says Mum and gives Oscar a hug.

What's your favourite food?

At breakfast the next day Oscar is still thinking about his Dad and the crash.

He says, "why did my Dad have to get hurt? I liked my Dad when he didn't shout and get tired."

"I know," says Mum, "but now your Dad has more time to read books with you and make boats."

Oscar feels happy he and his Dad can still have nice times together.

What do you like doing with your Dad?

9

Samuel is having tea with his Mum. He is sad. He is worried about Oscar's Dad.

"Oscar said his Dad's brain injury won't get better," Samuel says.

"I know," says Samuel's Mum. "Oscar's Dad might not go back to how he was before his crash, but he can still do lots of great things with Oscar!"

Samuel feels happy that Oscar's Dad can keep making great boats.

What makes you feel worried?

Dad is cross. Oscar's sister Josie has got paint on the chair.

Dad shouts at Josie and says bad words.

Josie cries. Mum and Oscar feel upset.

When Dad has gone upstairs, Oscar says, "it frightens me when Dad shouts at us, I don't think he loves us anymore."

What frightens you?

"No," says Mum, "Dad shouts because of his brain injury, it is not your fault. He still loves you very much."

Dad comes downstairs and is not shouting anymore. Mum gets some homemade cake and lemonade. They all eat it and everyone feels happy again.

What makes you feel happy?

Today is Father's Day. Mrs Rutter asks the children about their Dads.

Oscar and Samuel like Mrs Rutter, she is kind. The teacher gives them all pieces of card cut in different shapes.

"Write something nice about your Dad," says Mrs Rutter.

Did you do anything for your Dad on Father's Day?

Samuel writes, "my Dad runs fast."

Georgina writes, "my Dad reads me stories, I love stories."

Oscar writes, "my Dad makes great boats."

They all stick their pictures on a big poster. The poster says, "our Dads are great".

Write something nice about your Dad.

Tomorrow is the children's boat race.

Oscar's Dad is helping Oscar and Samuel to finish their boats.

Oscar's Dad says, "Samuel, don't forget to put on the sail, we want your boat to go faster than it did last year!"

Why don't you try and build a boat?

The race is nearly over and Oscar and Samuel are waiting at the bridge to see which boat is going to win.

"It's a draw!" shouts Mrs Rutter. Samuel and Oscar are both the winners.

"Our boats got to the bridge at the same time," Oscar tells his Dad.

"Thank you, you make great boats!" Samuel says to Oscar's Dad.

"I think so too," laughs Oscar

Who is your best friend?

Spot the Difference

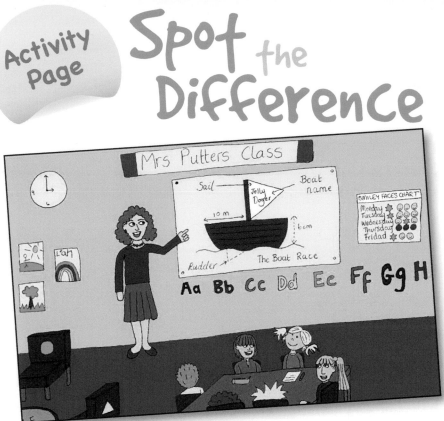

Can you spot the 11 differences?

Wordsearch

Activity Page

T	R	M	U	R	B	E	R	E	C	C	R	H	B
R	M	R	I	A	H	C	L	E	E	H	W	S	Z
A	G	N	I	S	S	E	C	O	R	P	B	F	X
U	I	A	N	I	A	R	B	S	E	B	O	L	R
M	O	G	J	C	L	N	S	L	B	K	K	S	Y
A	I	R	U	O	Q	A	Y	L	E	I	C	L	R
B	F	O	R	G	E	T	F	U	L	T	H	S	E
I	I	T	Y	N	M	T	R	R	L	E	E	Y	G
L	A	C	E	I	O	E	G	A	U	T	C	M	R
I	B	O	X	T	T	N	M	O	M	E	L	P	U
T	I	D	I	I	I	T	H	O	U	G	H	T	S
Y	C	R	R	V	O	I	H	Q	R	K	M	O	K
H	E	D	A	E	N	O	Z	C	F	Y	N	M	J
L	M	H	A	M	S	N	E	K	O	R	T	S	D

Brain	Injury	Forgetful
Cognitive	Emotions	Organ
Thoughts	Cells	Surgery
Trauma	Symptoms	Attention
Memory	Ability	Processing
Stroke	Cerebellum	Doctor
Cerebrum	Wheelchair	Lobes

19

Draw a picture of your family

All about me...

My Name is

These are the people in my family

Colour the shape below in your favourite colour

The colour of my eyes is

Draw your house in the cloud below

Draw your favourite food on the plate below

I don't like eating...

All about my Dad...

Here are some facts about
my Dad...

Draw a picture of your Dad doing
his favourite thing in
the box below

Name ....

Hair colour ....

Eye colour ....

Birthday ....

Favourite animal ....

Favourite sport ....

He really doesn't like...

Think of something you could do
to make your Dad smile and
write it in the cloud below

Does your Dad have a favourite
thing he often says? Write it in
the speech bubble below!

Spot the Difference Answers

1 Mrs "Putters Class" written on board

2 Clock hand shortened

3 10M boat measurement not 10cm

4 Orange not yellow sun on drawing on wall

5 Mrs Rutter has pink bead on necklace

6 Holly has no lips!

7 Georgina's hair bobble is a different colour

8 Name on boat on poster "Jolly Doger"

9 Reward Chart extra red face

10 "Fridad!" instead of "Friday" on reward chart

11 Left top Drawing pin on poster coloured black

Notes